Hello! My name is Skye Avalyn and I am the author and illustrator of this book. If you have decided to read my poems, I would just like to thank you for giving me a chance! I put a lot of work into creating this book and it gave me a lot of motivation and joy for life.

I have struggled with depression for as long as I can remember. Being diagnosed fairly recently marked a big change in my life where I started to get the help that I needed instead of bottling up all of my emotions and hating who I am.

Learning how to handle my mental illness came with a lot of new coping skills. Poetry and art are two major skills that help me ground myself and calm down.

I encourage any reader who has picked up this book to learn what they enjoy most in life and be able to do such things. I really hope that anyone who reads this collection of poems will find happiness and overcome any obstacles they face.

Thank you for giving this seventeen year old a chance, and enjoy! <3

# FLOWER GRAVEYARD

Begging for a drip of water
Something to get through the day
Hoping it's not a bother
There is no other water source, no other way

The leaves shriveling
The roots hiding
The petals falling

The flower suffers without any supporters
Only the soil will remain
Lifetime keeps getting shorter and shorter
Due to the lack of any rain

The flower travels to the graveyard
Alone and miserable
Wondering why it was so easy to discard
The flower's thoughts during the journey are
indecipherable

There's no way to go back
Should the flower have known?
Allowed itself to provide anything it lacked,
But, its last chance was blown
The second it didn't come up with another plan
And then the afterlife began

The flower graveyard
Filled with the ones that lost hope
Of ever helping themselves, of being able to grow

# THE LIGHT SWITCH DOESN'T WORK

I try, I try, I try again
Losing hope as it gets more dim

Worry becomes fear
As everything becomes less clear
I try to recall how I can get past it all
I ask, is it still nighttime?
For the darkness will never resign

I try, I try, I try again
Why couldn't it all just make sense?

Everything that I hold dear
I hear the whispers in my ear
Feeling so small, struggling to reach the switch as I crawl
I ask, will I ever hear the church bells chime?
As the beads of sweat on my forehead shine

I try, I try, I try again
Thinking about my dreams, my family, my friends
Looking in the mirror
I just want it all to disappear
Stumbling from wall to wall
I lose sight of my surroundings and withdrawal
I ask, can I ever get back what was once mine?
Or is it gone forever, lost in the trial of time

I tried, I tried, I tried again
I hope my messages will someday send

The darkness engulfs me as I am wondering
Why could no one mention that the light switch is
broken

I tried, I tried, I tried again
Flipping the switches until the end

# SECOND CHANCES

Knock knock knock
I hear you at my door
Knock knock knock
Curious of what this visit is for

Ruminating before I answer
To let you back in is to risk it all
But then, considering all the factors
Without you I feel so small

Infinite instances of the hurt you've brought
Maybe it's my own fault that I am filled with these
thoughts
Why do I associate your company with both the pain and
joy I have felt
The things I would do to stop the knocks and the chime
of the doorbell

The future is the furthest thing from my mind
The past as well, the passage of time slows
To let you in, I feel inclined
We can chat for a bit and see where it goes

I think to myself, how could you hurt me anymore?
So I grant your millionth last chance, and open the door.

## CONTROL

I long to be able to control what I feel
To know what it's like to not be alone
l know the torment I subject myself to is real
At a time where much of myself is unknown

All I desire is to understand the agony within
But that is out of my rule
And so I begin
The blade grazing across my skin is what I control

Stumbling through the bitter expanse of my mind
Unsure of what is real, of what power I have
In my own head it feels like I am blind
But that unknown part of me is all that is left
Following hurting myself time after time

The inner turmoil that I feel
I try to understand but it seems so inaccessible
Almost like the structure around my mind is made of
steel
Preventing me from getting in, from feeling acceptable

Control
Such a simple concept yet impossible to obtain
Out of my reign is the soul
Constantly trying to escape one's brain
All I want is to feel like I am whole

## LOVE YOURSELF FIRST

To love others before yourself, I view skeptically
As the contradictory desire
To feel wanted spoils credibility
I thought I could put others first, years prior
Despite my lack of capability
From being filled internally with barbed wire

However, it is unfair in many ways
Not only to yourself, but everyone involved
Hurt by the environment you offer praise
The negative perception remains unsolved

Until another person comes along
And gives you a chance to feel wanted
Fixing yourself is only prolonged
It's unavoidable, yet I am haunted
With my own sense of right and wrong

With them, they foster attachment
While what you see is a good support system
You burden them with every fragment
Until they become another victim


Of your own self-hatred.

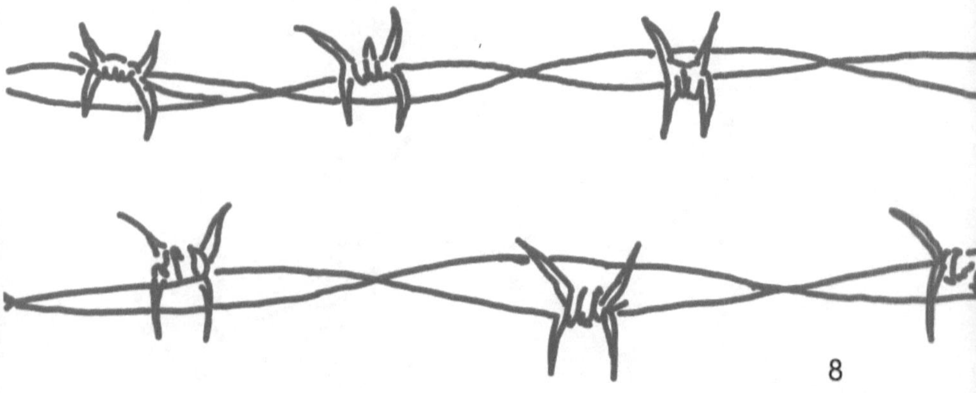

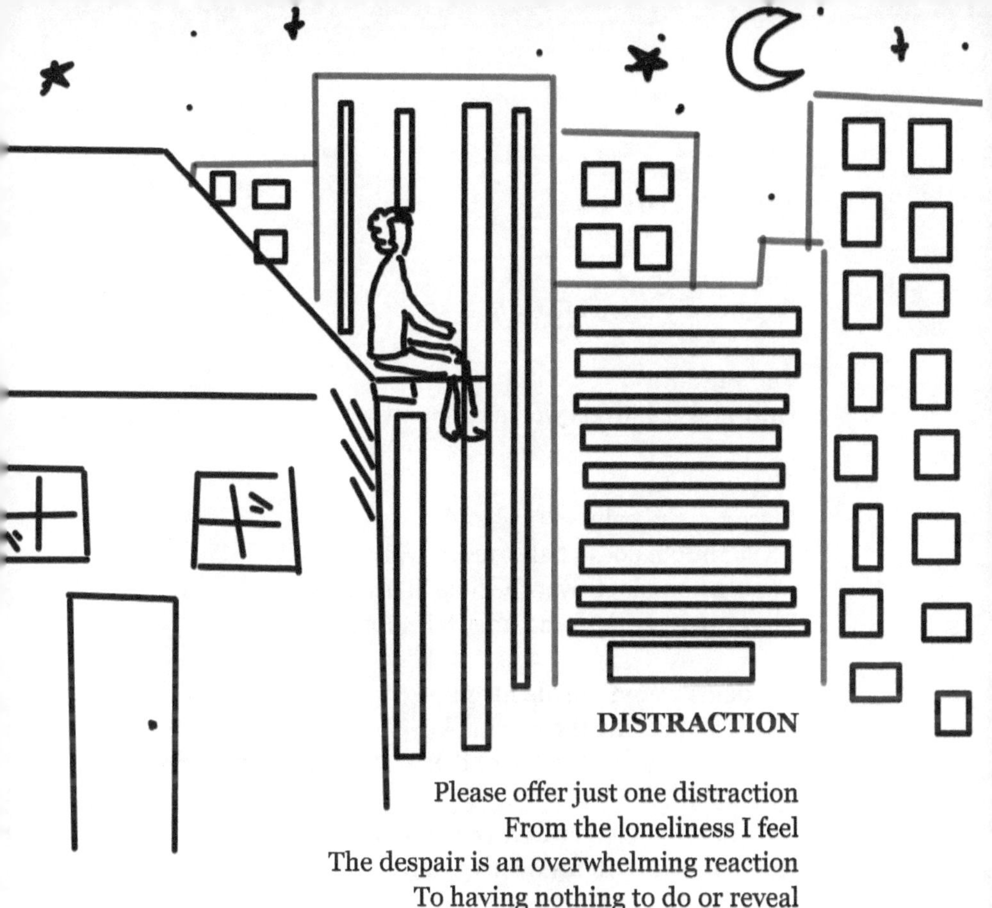

## DISTRACTION

Please offer just one distraction
From the loneliness I feel
The despair is an overwhelming reaction
To having nothing to do or reveal

Please distract me from my mind
It feels like the bones of my skull are confining me
To the emotions I was assigned
Please give me a break
Stuck like a fly in a spider web
Nowhere to go, nothing to fake

There is no escape at the end of the day
The clock ticks and time does not stop
Everyday I wish it was doomsday
I just sit on the rooftop
And dream about the end of it all

**THE ANTIDOTE**

The antidote
Supposedly there to help

The antidote
Only makes me feel worse about myself

The antidote
Placed in the palm of my hand
The antidote doesn't always work as planned
I put the bandage over the hole in my boat
They ask how it's doing, they take notes

Bandaids weren't made for ships
They can prolong the inevitable
But I watch as each piece of the boat breaks away, strip
by strip
The time will come where the antidote isn't helpful
And I am stuck in my own apocalypse

Water seeps around the edges of the bandaid
I halfheartedly convince them that it's okay when it's not
This was a game well played
Between me and the current I fought

I just want to be set free
From the potential to drown
All I ask for is the key
To understanding why the boat is going down

The water continues to come through
There's nothing I can do
Except understand that this is my fate
And this will be my permanent state

# DESERVING

The desire to feel love
Almost as if I deserve so
Trying to do things I am proud of
It will never fulfill me I know

I search for the intimacy I deserve
Which could be the absence of love,
Like warmth itself is reserved
And only rewarded to those worthy
Those who have earned their ticket to the Above

I envy those who feel the warmth of compassion
While I sit in the dark, unable to even give love to myself
Unable to take action
Regardless of if the change I make is heartfelt
I'm stuck in the never ending cycle of feeling like a
fraction

I've never felt whole
Never believed I was enough
Knowing the cycle will continue to torment my soul
I already expect to make my own life rough

**BALANCE**

I am walking down a tightrope
Each step takes me closer to the end
The steadiness is temporary
On this rope, my whole life depends
I walk along the tightrope
Scared to look below
But at the same time
Maybe the easiest choice would be to let go

**DAYDREAM**

An escape from our harsh and cold reality
Frivolous concepts and ideas flow through the mind
A limitless realm filled with every possibility
Leaving behind the person I would describe as a nobody
Yet, if I stay here I will fall behind
So what do I value more
To flee from life or to learn how to accept mankind?

## BIGGEST FEAR

Snakes, spiders, rodents too
These are just a few
There are many more
But solitude is what frightens you
And what shakes you to your core
Being alone means being with yourself
Which you are not ready for

## DELICATE

To keep everything to yourself is a disservice
To overshare is a burden
A thin line separates the two
To retain a delicate balance from person to person
What is needed is a breakthrough
Keeping to yourself versus telling your whole story
Oh, what should I do?

## REDISCOVERY

On the road to discovering who I am
Covered by the masks I've created
Feels like this is how I was programmed
Hidden is anything unrelated
To the person I claim to be
Past my disguise, no one can see
All the facades I've perfected
My true self I have neglected
Unsure of what I enjoy
Who am I without the decoy?
I ask myself each night
Trying to understand my soul
In an attempt to rewrite
All the experiences I've had to unroll

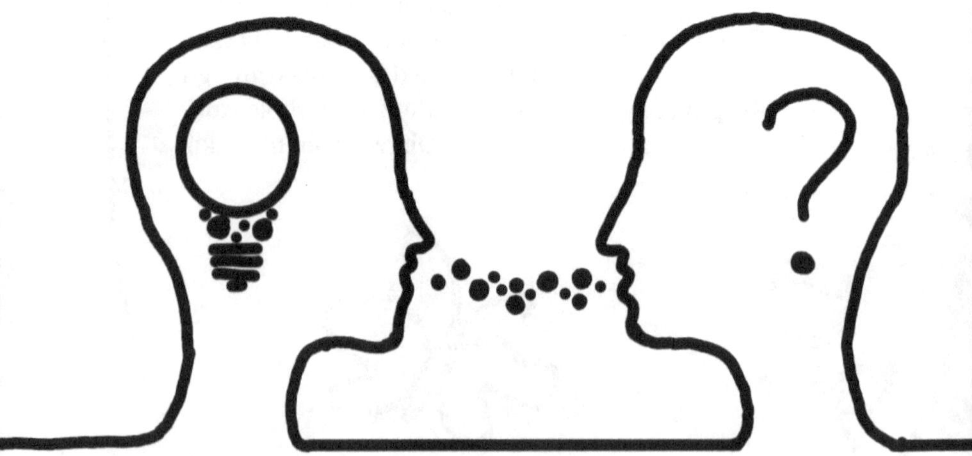

## HAPPINESS FEELS SELFISH

Episode after episode
Time passes by slow
I feel selfish for my own satisfaction
I would rather help others with my actions
Than have this gift I was bestowed
I hate to waste, I hate to loathe
I have to tell myself
That I am allowed to be happy,
I'm allowed to take up space,
And you are deserving too, in any case

## THERE'S ALWAYS ROOM

Self-improvement can always be necessary
Even in a person filled with complete satisfaction
While some may believe the contrary
Most people could use a distraction
From the hubbub we hear everyday
Everyone faces their own obstacles
I open the paper and read article after article
Of another "satisfied" person going away

## VALIDATION

In such a state
I lack the skills to self-validate
I rely on others to tell it to me straight
Yet at the same time I fear my fate
Living in a constant search of validation
My mind feels submerged
No compliment can make me feel elation
But I feel the energy in me surge
When I see a new source of validation emerge

My life is out of my hands
I need someone else to tell me I am valuable
For thinking so myself I am unable
I'm sure my efforts are admirable
But nothing will make me feel less damned

**PUZZLE**

I bought a puzzle the other day
Hoping it would help me cope in some way
I spent hours putting all the pieces together
Some pieces are missing I discover
It feels like all of my hard work is gone
As a puzzle isn't even something I can count on

I think a little more
And realize this puzzle is something I care for
Even if a few pieces aren't there
The capture of my boredom was rare

My effort is still valid
And it made me feel talented
Even if I'll never completely finish
Nothing can be done to diminish
The hope I feel
When I see a puzzle can be beautiful
Without every single piece

## RELIGION

The world offers comfort through gods
While it could just be deception
I believe there is an exception
Against all the odds
I believe everyone is guided by their perception
Believing in a higher power gives hope
And inspires people to manifest
Whatever they need to cope

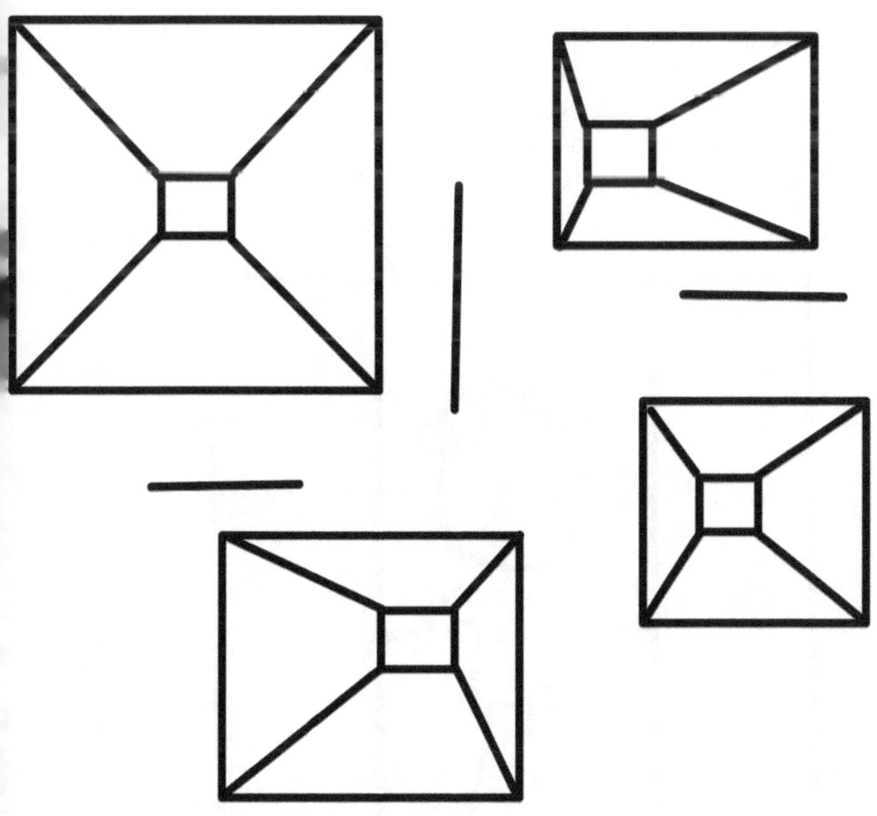

# STICKY SITUATION

Stuck between two walls
Do I value trust or honesty more?
I can keep one's trust in place
By keeping a secret from the other
Or I could be loyal and honest
And tell the other face-to-face
Then, I would lose the trust I value
As soon as one's steps are retraced
And my inability to keep secrets is uncovered


Either way I will leave a wall behind
So I must settle the case
Rather than being confined
To such a small and cramped place

## TREE ROOTS

I grew and I grow
Reaching up higher each time
My branches extend
I can clearly feel the wind flow

I grew and I grow
My roots expanding in the ground
Getting jumbled with nearby flowers and weeds
Not every tangle benefits me though

I grew and I grow
It takes years to unravel
The unnecessary tangles that hinder my growth
I have to fully understand them to be able to let go

I grew and I grow

## BROKEN

A baseball crashes into the living room
It frightens me and so I go under my bed
Held to my chest is a broom
If someone comes near, I can whack them in the head

In the hours following I wait and I wait
Having heard no noises I feel free
To go downstairs and see the chaos that awaits
I bring the broom to help to some degree

I walk down each step on the stairs
Terrified to make a sound
Yet once I arrived downstairs and I was aware
I laughed at how silly I was to not look around

The window was broken
But that can be fixed
But what about me, I had spoken
My progress, I become affixed

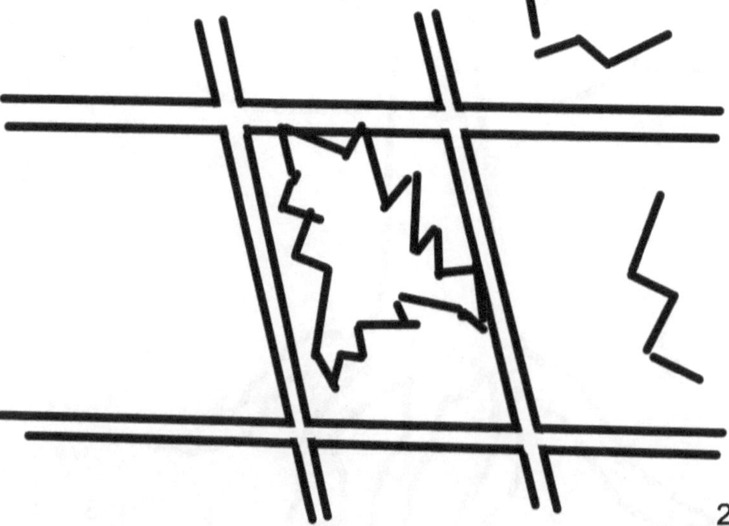

## VINES

Walking through the forest
Seeing the animals, I feel like a tourist
I start to feel drowsy
And my thoughts are getting cloudy
Maybe I should just lay down here
I can remain quiet so the creatures come near

Unexpectedly, so do the vines
They circle around me, I feel confined
Yet also welcome
As the vines start to beckon

They wrap around my legs, my back, my wrists
I never expected this walking into the forest
Now I am one with nature
Maybe I'll try to get up later


But for now, I just want to stay here.

## GONE

The light flickers
The candle melts
And the rain stops

How much I wish
I could go back
To when the wax was at the top

Longing for
An elusive feeling
Why can't it be nonstop

## SOULMATE

For much of our past
Fnd for as long as our lives last
You will always be beside me
Our souls connected as you expect them to be
Our stories are yet a draft

## STUCK

While everyone around me grows
I seem to be stuck in one place
And as I look up at all of those
Blooming flowers with a strong base
I think about all the times I'm
Being broken down leaf by leaf
They blossom while I'm frozen in time
Filled to my breaking point with grief
I'm in fall and everyone else is in spring
Their roots expand and mine shrink
Everyone thrives and I'm just slipping
Any new sprout goes away in a blink

# RAIN

Pitter patter on the roof
The constant noise makes me feel aloof
Droplets slide run down the windowpane
Doing their own little dance
As I join them and around I prance

Hoping the rain will stay
And be able to keep me safe
I run outside to enjoy the petrichor
And other delights outside my door

Dancing in the rain
With no cares in the world
I try to capture the moment in vain
As each new drop makes the puddles swirl

**PETALS**

To be or not to be
I ask the flower to tell me
Petal by petal
Fate is left to each flower that's special
Buttercups, peonies, roses too
All make me wonder if I'm meant to be with you
The petals drop
Nothing asking them to stop
I get my answer and I go
Leaving a trail of flower petals to the places I know

## COLOR OUTSIDE THE LINES

Coloring pages
The hubris of a perfectionist
Rather than relax the artist rages
At any part where the paper looks hectic

Unable to let go of the desire
To be perfect, to be the best
The perfectionist's situation is dire
As they can't settle for anything less

## SOUVENIR

An object capturing a treasured moment
From different destinations
This souvenir was the one chosen
Out of all the options on that vacation

While it may not hold any significance within itself
The holder of the treasure understands it's wealth
It may mean nothing to someone new
But it means everything to those it is given to

It represents the desire to feel wanted
As the vacationer saw it fit to get you a gift
It means your friendship is solid

# COMFORT

Comfort is light pink and pale yellow like the colors of
blossoming flowers
Found in the taste of gelato on a summer night, even if it
is a bit sour
Breathing in the subtle scent of cologne on Dad's sweater
It looks like a smile from a stranger or a personal letter
The mellow sound of rain sprinkling outside while
playing games with friends
Comfort is the warmth from enveloping someone
familiar in a tight hug when all of this ends

## SADNESS

Sadness is an inescapable expanse of the deepest shade
of blue
It tastes like the flavor of chips for dinner when there's
no motivation to cook something new
The scent of the pillow when sleeping from noon till the
middle of the night
It looks like that unfamiliar person on the other side of
the mirror who never quite looks right
After a call with a friend ends, the silence that follows
Sadness is when the tears are coming and it feels
impossible to swallow

## MOTIVATION

New accomplishments are what I desire
Yet my head stays on my pillow
All I do is prop it up a little higher
I can't seem to get out of bed
No matter how hard I try, I can never acquire
The strength nor motivation to get up
To overcome feeling tired
My inability to get up only complements
The constant worry I already felt prior

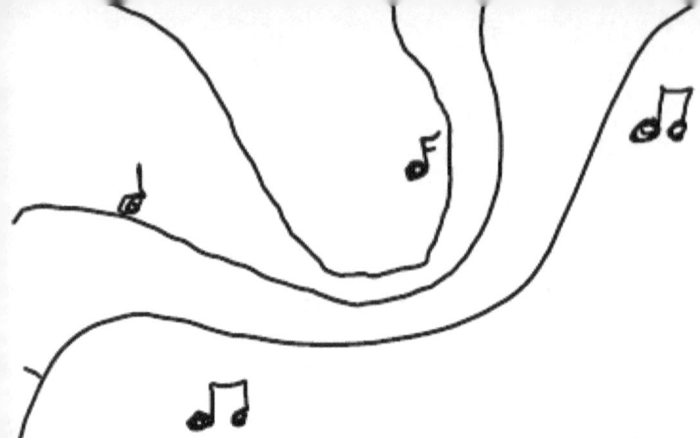

## SOUNDS

There are footsteps in the distance
Muffled voices somewhere near
I struggle to remain calm
When my awareness comes from my ears
Worrying that I'm being watched
That someone is right outside my door
I worry about every noise
It truly shakes me to my core

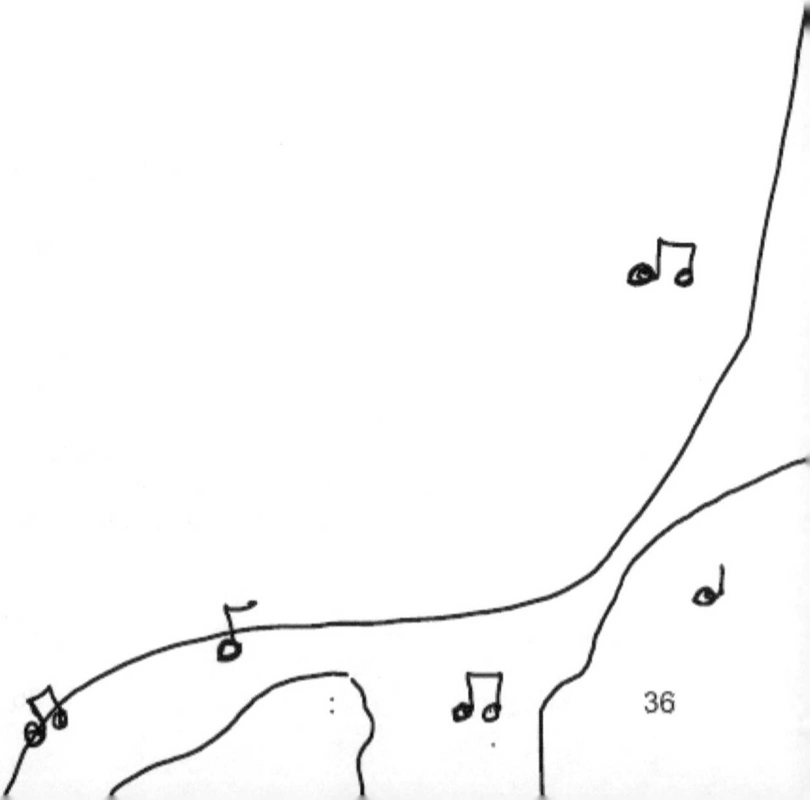

**THE OCEAN**

The vast expanse of water
Extending further than I can possibly see
I admire the scenic view
But if I'm being honest, the ocean scares me
Fear of the unknown
Drives me to stay on the sand
Safe and secure on the shore's land

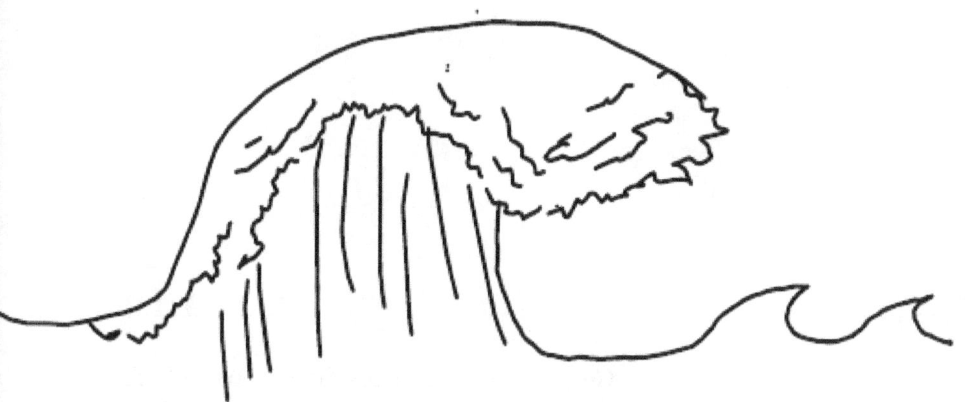

## LAUGHTER

Genuine laughter is my favorite part of life
Hearing others enjoy themselves
Makes the world seem so very bright

**GROUP**

Letting others in
Telling them the truth
They know what you've done, where you've been
What's been hidden since your youth

To let them know
Requires the greatest strength of all
To let them help you grow
To stop putting up your wall

The mask slowly fades
And vulnerability shines through
As you show all of your shades
Anger, depression, anxiety too

Letting them in is up to you.

## DEFENSE

The heart is protected
A new layer added each time it breaks
One day its strength will be perfected
One day you won't feel it ache

The brain in which it is connected
Tries to lay on the brakes
Preventing you from getting infected
With any more heartache

## SURFACE LEVEL

All of those little moments
Create a false truth about life
Even when you are at your lowest
Even when you grab the knife

It feels like happiness
Surely it could be
There are many friends to witness
The "you" that seems so carefree

Surface level happiness
Seems to eliminate the possibility of the bad
Yet, it takes someone fearless
To recognize that truly feeling happy
Requires work on what makes you sad

True, deeply felt joy
Seems so out of reach
Living off the temporary memories
They make you happy, you preach

However, happiness comes from inside
Not from external factors
Sadness is not something you can so easily hide
It takes patience to finish this chapter
I believe it will come in time

What is the cow thinking?

Hell if I moo [knew]!

Thanks for reading. MWAH!